THIS BOOK BELONGS TO

_____

GUESS THE 8000M MOUNTAIN

1. This mountain stands at 8586m and borders Nepal and China. It was first climbed in 1955.

2. This mountain is the smallest of the fourteen official 8000er's standing at 8013m. It was also the last of the 8000m mountains to be climbed due to its location being entirely in Tibet.

3. This mountain is on the border of China and Pakistan and is the 12th highest mountain in the world at 8047m. It was first ascended in 1957.

4. This mountain stands at 8848m. The first official ascent came in 1953.

5. This mountain is the fifth tallest in the world standing at 8463m. It is an isolated peak which borders Nepal and Tibet.

6. This mountain is the 13th highest mountain in the world standing at 8035m. It is in the Karakorum range, and shares the same name as one of the other mountains on the list.

7. This mountain is the 10th highest mountain in the world standing at 8091m. Despite being among the most treacherous mountains in the world, this mountain was the first 8000m mountain to be ascended in 1950 and is the only 8000'er to be successfully climbed on the first try.

8. This mountain is the fourth highest in the world standing at 8516m. It is part of the Everest massif, and is connected to the south col.

9. This mountain is the sixth highest mountain in the world standing at 8188m. It's name means turquoise goddess in Tibetan.

10. This mountain is the seventh highest mountain in the world standing at 8167m. It is the highest mountain within the borders of a single country (Nepal), and its first ascent was in 1960.

11. This mountain is the eleventh highest mountain on the list standing at 8068m. This mountain is the highest in its massif, and also shares a name with another mountain on the list.

12. This mountain is the ninth highest mountain in the world standing at 8126m. It is the western most 8000m mountain and known to be a difficult climb.

13. This mountain is the eighth highest mountain in the world standing at 8163m. It's name means '*mountain of the spirit*', and is described from the Sanskrit word manasa meaning intellect.

14. This mountain stands at 8611m above sea level. It is located on the China-Pakistan border, and is the highest mountain in the Karakoram range.

'WE DO NOT LIVE TO EAT AND MAKE MONEY. WE EAT AND MAKE MONEY TO BE ABLE TO LIVE. THAT IS WHAT LIFE MEANS AND WHAT LIFE IS FOR'

–MALLORY

Lhotse and Everest

HIGHEST MOUNTAIN IN EACH CONTINENT

(excluding Asia because that's too easy)

1. This mountain is in Tanzania, near to the Kenyan border. It stands 5895m above sea level and is the tallest mountain in its continent.

2. This mountain is the highest in Europe. This extinct volcano was formed 2.5 million years ago and stands at 5642m.

3. This mountain is in the centre of the Alaska range and is the tallest in its continent. It stands at 6190m above sea level and is considered to be the third most isolated peak in the world.

4. This mountain is in Chile and is the highest mountain in the Southern hemisphere. It stands at 6959m above sea level and was first ascended in 1897.

5. This mountain is the highest peak in Antarctica and was first discovered in 1958. It stands at 4892m above sea level and was named after a US congressman.

6. This mountain is the highest peak in Australasia. It is on the Indonesian island of New Guinea, and it stands at 4884m above sea level.

7. This mountain is considered by many to be the highest of its continent although it is a bit of a grey area. It stands at 4810m above sea level and has a tunnel going through it.

8. This mountain is the second highest in North America and is the highest peak in Canada. It stands at 5959m above sea level and was named after a Canadian geologist. What is it called?

   a. Mount Peter   b. Mount Logan   c. Mount Raymond   d. Mount Clayton

9. This mountain is the second highest peak in South America standing at 6893m above sea level. It is the highest active volcano in the world and is located in Chile. What is it called?

   a. Ojos del Dorada   b. Ojos del Comares   c. Ojos del Finito   d. Ojos del Salado

10. This mountain stands at 4852m above sea level and is the second highest peak in Antarctica. As of 2017 the summit had only been reached on six occasions by fifteen different people. What is it called?

   a. Mount Tyree   b. Mount Shinn   c. Mount Gardner   d. Mount Markham

11. Standing at 5199m, what is the second highest mountain in Africa?

   a. Mount Ghana   b. Mount Nigeria   c. Mount Guinea   d. Mount Kenya

12. What is the fourth highest mountain in Australasia that stands at 3724m above sea level and is in New Zealand?

13. What is the name of North America's third highest mountain?

   a. Pico de Orizaba   b. Pico de Kurzawa   c. Pico de Boli

'THE SUMMIT IS WHAT DRIVES US, BUT THE CLIMB ITSELF IS WHAT MATTERS'
-ANKER

Mont Blanc

FIRST ASCENTS

1. In 1924 two mountaineers attempted to climb Everest, and some speculate whether they were successful in reaching the summit before their death. What are the names of the two mountaineers?

2. In what year was Mont Blanc first climbed by Michael Gabriel Paccard and Jacques Balmat?

   a. 1686   b. 1726   c. 1756   d. 1786

3. What is the name of the climber who attempted one of the first ascents of the Eiger north face in 1936 but was tragically unsuccessful? After the rest of his team died, he attempted to abseil down by himself but froze to death because of a knot in his rope to be too big to get through his carabiner.

4. When was the Eiger north face first climbed?

   a. 1937   b. 1938   c. 1939   d. 1940

5. When was the first ascent of K2?

   a. 1954   b. 1956   c. 1958   d. 1960

6. What nationality were the team that first ascended Aconcagua in 1896?

   a. French   b. British   c. German   d. Austrian

7. What is the name of the famous ridge that overlooks the north face of the Eiger, which was first climbed in 1921?

8. Nanga Parbat became the second 8000m mountain to be climbed. This solo feat was achieved by Hermann Buhl. In what year did he climb the mountain?

   a. 1950   b. 1952   c. 1953   d. 1955

9. Name the mountain that was first climbed in 1959 by Maestri and Egger and is dubbed the 'hardest mountain in the world'. It can be found in a region that is disputed between Argentina and Chile.

10. Which Brit lead the party that first ascended the Matterhorn in 1865?

11. Mount Vinson was astonishingly only first discovered in 1958. Nicholas Clinch would later go on to lead the first team to ascend the mountain, but in what year was this achieved?

    a. 1960   b. 1962   c. 1964   d. 1966

12. The first official ascent of Everest was in 1953. Name the two climbers who achieved this feat.

13. Frederick Cook claimed the first ascent of Mount Mckinley (Denali) in 1906 but this ascent is unverified, and its legitimacy questioned. When was the first official ascent?

    a. 1907   b. 1909   c. 1911   d. 1913

14. Despite being climbed over 10,000 times every year the first ascent of Ben Nevis came surprisingly late. When was Britain's highest mountain first officially climbed?

    a. 1645   b. 1705   c. 1771   d. 1824

15. In what year did Luchsinger and Reiss first climb Lhotse?

    a. 1954   b. 1956   c. 1958   d. 1959

'IT IS NOT THE MOUNTAIN WE CONQUER, BUT OURSELVES'

-HILLARY

The Eiger

THE ALPS

1. What is the third highest mountain in the Alps standing at 4545m above sea level?

2. The Alps are generally divided into the Western and Eastern Alps. Which side of the Alps has the higher summits?

3. How high is Monte Rosa?

    a. 4711   b. 4686   c. 4664   d. 4634

4. How many 4000er's are there in the Alps?

    a. 64   b. 75   c. 82   d. 90

5. There are five mountains in the Alps above 4500m. Mont Blanc, Monte Rosa, Dom, Lyskamm and what other mountain?

6. What is the name of the highest mountain in Germany standing at 2962m above sea level?

7. Grossglockner is the highest mountain in Austria, but how high is it?

    a. 3998   b. 3845   c. 3798   d. 3754

8. What is the name of the mummified man that was found in 1991 at the Austrian/Italian border?

9. What percentage of Europe's area does the Alps make up?

   a. 4%   b. 6%   c. 8%   d. 11%

10. How many countries do the Alps spread across?

    a. 6   b. 7   c. 8   d. 9

11. What is the name of the indigenous goat that lives in the Alps?

12. What is the name of the ninth highest mountain in the Alps which has the second largest glacier on it, and is the highest mountain in the Bernese Alps?

13. What is the name of the mountain that is attached to Aiguille Verte, and is famous for its sheer rock faces?

14. Finish the name of the mountain that stands at 4208m above sea level. Grandes _____

15. What is the name of the longest glacier in the Alps?

'THE MOUNTAINS ARE CALLING AND I MUST GO'
-MUIR

The Matterhorn

GENERAL KNOWLEDGE

1. If you were trekking in the high Tatras, which country would you be in?

    a. Slovenia   b. Russia   c. Slovakia   d. Hungary

2. Regularly smouldering Mount Shishaldin is regarded as the world's most perfectly conical volcano. Which country is it in?

    a. Nepal   b. Japan   c. Austria   d. United States

3. Which is the world's longest mountain range?

    a. The Andes   b. The Himalayas   c. The Alps   d. The Transarctic Mountains

4. When asked why he wanted to climb Mount Everest, who said 'because it's there'?

5. In Scotland, a Munro is a mountain that is...

    a. Over 1100m   b. Top 100 mountains in the country   c. Over 3000 feet

6. Khan Tengri (meaning King Heaven) is the world's most northerly 7,000m-plus peak. Which country is it in?

    a. Mongolia   b. Kazakhstan   c. Vietnam   d. Canada

7. Which of these famous mountains is the lowest?

   a. The Matterhorn   b. Mount Olympus   c. Mount Kosciuszko   d. Mount Fuji

8. And which of these famous peaks is the highest?

   a. Kilimanjaro   b. Mont Blanc   c. Mount Elbrus   d. Mount Whitney

9. Which of these volcanos is not part of the pacific ring of fire?

   a. Krakatoa   b. Mount St Helens   c. Mount Fuji   d. Mount Pelée

10. What is the most climbed mountain in the world, with around 300,000 ascents every year?

    a. Mount Fuji   b. Snowdon   c. Mont Blanc   d. Ben Nevis

11. Which mountain range extends from the Grampians to the Cape York Peninsula?

    a. The Alps   b. The Appalachians   c. The Pennines   d. The Great Dividing Range

12. Where can the volcano Mauna Kea be found?

'LIFE'S A BIT LIKE MOUNTAINEERING, NEVER LOOK DOWN'
–HILLARY

Annapurna

BRITISH MOUNTAINS

1. True or false. Arthur's Seat in Holyrood Park, Edinburgh is a hill of volcanic origin?

2. What is the second highest mountain in Great Britain?

3. How high is Ben Nevis?

    a. 1285m   b. 1315m   c. 1345m   d. 1405m

4. The Cotswolds are mainly in which English county?

    a. Devon   b. Cornwall   c. Gloucestershire   d. Yorkshire

5. How high is Snowdon?

    a. 985m   b. 1015m   c. 1045m   d. 1085m

6. How many official Munros are there in Scotland?

    a. 155   b. 193   c. 244   d. 282

7. What is the highest mountain in the England?

8. The Sperrin Mountains are in which country of the British Isles?

   a. Northern Ireland   b. England   c. Wales   d. Scotland

9. All of England's top 10 highest peaks can be found in one county in England. Which county is this?

10. In which county would you find the mountain range of Dartmoor?

    a. Cornwall   b. Somerset   c. Avon   d. Devon

11. How many mountains in Wales are above 1000m?

    a. 1   b. 2   c. 3   d. 4

12. The third highest mountain in England has a famous ridge called Striding Edge and stands at 950m above sea level. What is its name?

13. How many mountains above 900m are there in England?

   a. 4   b. 6   c. 8   d. 10

14. What is the fourth highest mountain in Scotland that has the first name Cairn?

   a. Gorm   b. Toul   c. Tay   d. Dame

15. What is the area called where the largest mountains in Wales are?

'EVERY MOUNTAIN TOP IS WITHIN REACH IF YOU JUST KEEP CLIMBING'
–FINLAY

Snowdonia

GUESS THE CLIMBING GEAR

1. What do you can attach to the bottom of your shoes, and are needed for walking on snow and glaciers?

2. This gear is used as an anchor in mountaineering. It is also driven into the ice and used to stop falls. They can also be placed horizontally in the snow as a deadman, which people can abseil from.

3. This is a knot or friction hitch that is used to attach a loop of chord around a rope. It has many uses such as in rock climbing, mountaineering, canyoneering and many more.

4. This is an electronic device that is worn on the body that helps the person to be found in the event that they are covered by an avalanche.

5. This is an oval shaped loop with a spring-loaded bar to keep it closed. It is often used to attach ropes together and thread ropes onto safety equipment.

6. These are large _____ shaped wedges of metal that you slot into constrictions in wider cracks, to provide protection when traditionally climbing outdoors. They can also be called Chocks, Cow bells, wedges or torque nuts.

7. This is a multi-purpose climbing tool that is used on both the ascent and descent of routes that involve frozen conditions and lots of snow. It can also be used in case of a fall to slow down and stop the person sliding down the mountain.

8. These are a cloth or leather leg coverings reaching from the instep to above the ankle or to mid-calf or knee. They prevent the shoes and feet from getting wet and are often worn when walking in snowy conditions.

9. These are thin wedges of metal that are slotted into constrictions in cracks to provide protection when climbing traditionally outdoors. They can also be called wires, rocks or stoppers.

10. This secures a person to a rope or an anchor point. It is essential for rock climbing and abseiling. In order to wear it, the climber loops the rope between their legs.

'PEOPLE DO NOT DECIDE TO BECOME EXTRAORDINARY. THEY DECIDE TO ACCOMPLISH EXTRAORDINARY THINGS'

−HILLARY

Ama Dablan

EVEREST

1. Jordan Romero became the youngest person to ever summit Everest in 2010, but how old was he?

    a. 12   b. 13   c. 14   c. 15

2. In 2013 a record number of climbers successfully reached the summit of Everest in a single year. How many was it?

    a. 485   b. 564   c. 658   d. 804

3. In 2004 the Sherpa Pemba Dorje set the record for the fastest climb of Everest from Base Camp to summit. What was his time?

    a. 6 hours 3 mins   b. 8 hours 10 mins   c. 9 hours 50 mins

4. What is the accepted height of Everest?

    a. 8842m   b. 8844m   c. 8846m   d. 8848m

5. Yuichiro Miura became the oldest person to summit Everest in 2013, but how old was he?

    a. 72   b. 76   c. 80   d. 84

6. Who was the first climber to solo summit Everest?

a. Stephen Venables   b. Tenzing Norgay   c. Reinhold Messner

7. Kami Rita Sherpa holds the record for the most ascents of Mount Everest. How many times has he reached the summit?

    a. 12 b. 16 c. 20 d. 24

8. What was Edmund Hillary's profession?

    a. Teacher b. Doctor c. Pro football player d. Beekeeper

9. As of August 2020, how many deaths have there been on Everest?

    a. 221 b. 268 c. 306 d. 358

10. Whose body was famously found on Mt. Everest in 1999?

11. What is the Tibetan name for mount Everest meaning 'mother goddess of the earth'?

12. How many metres above sea level is base camp at Everest?

    a. 5364m b. 5625m c. 5885m d. 6124m

13. Above what altitude are climbers considered to be in the 'death zone'?

14. Everest is widely considered to be the tallest mountain on earth, but there is one mountain that is taller if measured from the sea floor. What is the name of this mountain?

    a. Mauna Loa b. Mount Mckinley c. Cho Oyu d. Mauna Kea

'THE EXPERIENCED MOUNTAIN CLIMBER IS NOT INTIMIDATED BY A MOUNTAIN; HE IS INSPIRED BY IT'
-WARD

Everest

MOUNTAINEERING TRAGEDIES

1. In 1936 there was tragedy when four experienced German and Austrian climbers died trying to climb the Eiger north face. What is the name of the climber who has a traverse named after him on the Eiger?

   a. Kurz b. Hinterstoisser c. Angerer d. Rainer

2. In what year did the worst British mountaineering accident happen where five school children and one of their leaders tragically died in the Cairngorms due to bad weather?

   a. 1971 b. 1990 c. 1953 d. 1928

3. In 1974, an ill-equipped group of eight women tried to climb this 7134m peak. They were hit by bad weather at the summit and sadly all died on the descent. What is the name of the mountain that they were climbing?

a. Michael's Peak b. Salin Peak c. Khan Peak d. Lenin Peak

4. 1986 was the deadliest year in the history of K2, but how many lives did the mountain claim that year?

   a. 13 b. 14 c. 15 d. 16

5. What is the name of the mountain guide who died in 1996 on Everest after failing to meet his 2pm turnaround time? He tragically rang his wife whilst stranded near to the summit to tell her that he wasn't going to make it down.

6. 1996 was the deadliest year in the history of Everest but how many people died in this year?

   a. 10   b. 11   c. 13   d. 15

7. In 1934 there was a climbing tragedy when 10 people died on one of the 8000m mountains, which at the time was the worst mountaineering accident of all time. What mountain were they climbing?

   a. Everest   b. K2   c. Cho Oyu   d. Nanga Parbat

8. In 1865 Edward Whymper led the first team to summit the Matterhorn. The descent brought tragedy, however. How many people died on this climb?

   a. 2   b. 3   c. 4   d. 5

9. In 2019 three people tragically died and a fourth was injured on Ben Nevis. How were these people killed?

10. In 2014 there was a snowstorm that killed 43 people in the month of October, which included 21 trekkers. In which country did this tragedy happen?

    a. China   b. Peru   c. Nepal   d. Pakistan

'YOU ARE NOT IN
THE MOUNTAINS.
THE MOUNTAINS
ARE IN YOU'
—WEIR

Aiguille du Midi

GUESS THE MOUNTAIN

1. This mountain stands at 4478m above sea level and is on the border between Switzerland and Italy. It is famous for its distinctive pyramidal shape.

2. This is the tallest mountain in the solar system, and it is found on Mars. It is a very large shield volcano and stands at over 21,000m!

3. This volcano is located on the Gulf of Naples. It was responsible for destroying the Roman cities of Pompei, Herculaneum, Oplontis and Stabiae in 79 BC.

4. This volcano stands at 813m above sea level and can be found between the islands of Juva and Sumatra in Indonesia. This volcano had a very large eruption in 1883 that is estimated to have killed between 36000 to 120000 people.

5. This mountain stands at 3798m above sea level and is found in Austria. It is the highest mountain in the Alps east of the Ortler range, and after Mont Blanc has the second greatest topography isolation of all the mountains in the Alps.

6. What is the name of the 3000-foot granite wall that Alex Honald successfully climbed without the use of ropes in 2017?

7. This mountain stands at 4208m above sea level and can be found in the Mont Blanc massif. Its north face is considered to be one of the great three north faces in the alps along with the Eiger and the Matterhorn.

8. This mountain is notable for the ascent of its 'normal' route having the greatest vertical height gain from the valley of all the alpine mountains. Its name is a German word for cathedral.

9. This is the second highest mountain in England standing at 964m above sea level.

10. This volcano can be found in Iceland and stands at 1651m above sea level. This volcano erupted in 2010 causing massive disruption to air travel to Western and Eastern Europe for a week. (Its name is basically impossible to spell so you are a true mountain expert if you get it right!)

'MOUNTAINS ARE LIKE
THE GREAT EQUALIZER.
IT DOESN'T MATTER WHO
ANYONE IS OR WHAT
THEY DO'
−CHIN

Kilimanjaro

FAMOUS MOUNTAINEERS

1. This man was born in 1912 in Austria. He was part of the four-man climbing team that made the first ascent of the Eiger north face and wrote the books Seven Years in Tibet and the White Spider. He has alliteration between his first and second name.

2. This American man was born in 1955 and died on Everest in 1996. He was renowned for climbing 8000m peaks without oxygen being the first to achieve this feat on Lhotse. He was working for the Mountain Madness team in 1996 when he lost his life on Everest.

3. This American man was born in 1954. He is the author of best-selling books: Into Thin Air, Into The Wild and Under The Banner of Heaven. He was part of the ill fated 1996 Everest expedition but managed to survive.

4. This British man was born in 1840. He made many first ascents in regions such as: the Mont Blanc massif, South America, and the Rockies. He wrote the book Scrambles Amongst the Alps.

5. This Swiss climber was the first to solo Annapurna via the notoriously difficult south face. He won two Piolet d'Or awards in 2009 and 2014. He set many speed records on difficult faces

in the Alps such as the Eiger north face, but he sadly passed away in 2017 after a fall during an acclimatisation climb.

6. This Austrian man was born in 1942. He achieved many first ascents in the Rocky Mountains and was the first European to climb on the big walls in Yosemite National Park. He and Messner were the first two to climb Everest without supplemental oxygen.

7. This Polish woman with the first name Wanda was the first woman to summit K2, and the third woman to summit Everest.

8. This man was born in New Zealand in 1919. He climbed Everest in 1953 and, by 1958, he had reached both the north pole and the south pole making him the first person to achieve all three of these.

9. This Japanese woman was born in 1939. She is the first woman to reach the summit of Everest, and the first woman to ascend the seven summits.

10. This man is a professional rock climber specialising in lead climbing and bouldering. He was born in 1993 in the Czech Republic. He is the only male climber to have won the world cup series in both disciplines (lead climbing in 2009, 2015, 2019, and bouldering in 2010).

'THE HARDEST
MOUNTAIN TO
CLIMB IS THE ONE
WITHIN'
-LYNN

El Capitan

HIMALAYAS

1. Krzysztof Wielicki and Leszek Cichy became the first people to ascend Everest in the winter. What year did they achieve this feat in?

    a. 1964   b. 1969   c. 1975   d. 1980

2. Which of the 8000m mountains has the highest death percentage?

    a. Everest   b. K2   c. Lhotse   d. Annapurna

3. At the borders of which countries lies Everest?

4. What is the highest mountain in the Karakorum range?

    a. K2   b. Kanchenjunga   c. Lhotse   d. Makalu

5. What is the highest mountain in India?

    a. K2   b. Kanchenjunga   c. Makalu   d. Cho Oyu

6. What is the highest mountain in Pakistan?

    a. K2   b. Kanchenjunga   c. Makalu   d. Cho Oyu

7. From west to east, how far do the Himalayas stretch?

   a. 1045 miles   b. 1302 miles   c. 1550 miles   d. 1845 miles

8. There are three countries that have sovereignty over the Himalayas. Two of these three are India and Nepal but what is the third?

   a. China   b. Bhutan   c. Pakistan   d. India

9. What is the 15th highest mountain in the world, and the highest mountain below 8000m?

   a. Gyachung Chang   b. Gasherbrum III   c. Himalchuli

10. How many glaciers are located in the Himalayas?

    a. 5000   b. 10000   c. 15000   d. 20000

11. True or false? The Himalayas are regarded as a young mountain range.

12. What type of animal is Himalayan snow leopard most closely related to?

> 'LIFE SUCKS A LOT LESS WHEN YOU ADD MOUNTAIN AIR, A CAMPFIRE AND SOME PEACE AND QUIET'
>
> –HAMPTON

Sunset in the Himalayas

ANSWERS

GUESS THE 8000M MOUNTAIN

1. Kanchenjunga
2. Shishapangma
3. Broad Peak
4. Everest
5. Makalu
6. Gasherbrum II
7. Annapurna
8. Lhotse
9. Cho You
10. Dhaulagiri
11. Gasherbrum I
12. Nanga Parbat
13. Manaslu
14. K2

HIGHEST MOUNTAIN IN EACH CONTINENT

1. Mount Kilimanjaro
2. Mount Elbrus
3. Mount Mckinley (Denali)
4. Mount Aconcagua
5. Vinson Massif
6. Puncak Jaya
7. Mont Blanc
8. Mount Logan
9. Ojos del Salado
10. Mount Tyree
11. Mount Kenya
12. Mount Cook
13. Pico de Orizaba

FIRST ASCENTS

1. George Mallory and Andrew Irvine
2. 1786
3. Toni Kurz
4. 1938
5. 1954
6. British
7. Mittellegi
8. 1953
9. Cerro Torre
10. Edward Whymper
11. 1966
12. Tenzing Norgay and Edmund Hillary
13. 1913
14. 1771
15. 1956

THE ALPS

1. Dom
2. Western Alps
3. 4634
4. 82
5. Weisshorn
6. Zugspitze
7. 3798
8. Ötzi the Iceman
9. 11%
10. 8
11. Ibex
12. Finsteraarhron
13. Aiguille du Dru
14. Jorasses
15. Aletsch glacier (on Aletschhorn)

GENERAL KNOWLEDGE

1. Slovakia
2. United States
3. The Andes
4. George Mallory
5. Over 3000 feet
6. Kazakhstan
7. Mount Kosciuszko
8. Kilimanjaro
9. Mount Pelee
10. Mount Fuji
11. The Great Dividing Range
12. Hawaii

BRITISH MOUNTAINS

1. True
2. Ben Macdui
3. 1345m
4. Gloucestershire
5. 1085m
6. 282
7. Scafell Pike
8. Northern Ireland
9. Cumbria
10. Devon
11. 3
12. Helvellyn
13. 8
14. Toul
15. Snowdonia

NAME THE CLIMBING GEAR

1. Crampons
2. Snow Picket
3. Prusik
4. Avalanche transceiver
5. Carabiner
6. Climbing hexes
7. Ice Axe
8. Gaiters
9. Nuts
10. Harness

EVEREST

1. 13
2. 658
3. 8 hours and 10 minutes
4. 8848m
5. 80
6. Reinhold Messner
7. 24
8. Beekeeper
9. 306
10. George Mallory
11. Chomolungma
12. 5364m
13. Above 8000m
14. Mauna Kea

MOUNTAINEERING TRAGEDIES

1. Hinterstoisser
2. 1971
3. Lenin Peak
4. I3
5. Rob Hall
6. I5
7. Nanga Parbat
8. 4
9. Avalanche
10. Nepal

GUESS THE MOUNTAIN

1. Matterhorn
2. Olympos Mons
3. Mount Vesuvius
4. Krakatau
5. Grossglockner
6. El Capitan
7. Grande Jorasses
8. Dom
9. Scafell
10. Eyjafjallajökull

FAMOUS MOUNTAINEERS

1. Heinrich Harrer
2. Scott Fischer
3. Jon Krakauer
4. Edward Whymper
5. Ueli Steck
6. Peter Habeler
7. Wanda Rutkiewicz
8. Edmund Hillary
9. Junko Tabei
10. Adam Ondra

HIMALAYAS

1. 1980
2. Annapurna
3. Nepal and China
4. K2
5. Kanchenjunga
6. K2
7. 1550 miles
8. Bhutan
9. Gyachung Chang
10. 15000
11. True
12. Tiger

Printed in Great Britain
by Amazon